The Quotable
FARM DOG

MBI

First published in 2005 by MBI, an imprint of MBI Publishing Company, Galtier Plaza, Suite 200, 380 Jackson Street, St. Paul, MN 55101-3885 USA

© MBI Publishing Company, 2005

All rights reserved. With the exception of quoting brief passages for the purposes of review, no part of this publication may be reproduced without prior written permission from the Publisher.

The information in this book is true and complete to the best of our knowledge. All recommendations are made without any guarantee on the part of the author or Publisher, who also disclaim any liability incurred in connection with the use of this data or specific details.

This publication has been prepared solely by MBI Publishing Company and is not approved or licensed by any other entity. We recognize that some words, model names, and designations mentioned herein are the property of the trademark holder. We use them for identification purposes only. This is not an official publication.

MBI titles are also available at discounts in bulk quantity for industrial or sales-promotional use. For details write to Special Sales Manager at MBI Publishing Company, Galtier Plaza, Suite 200, 380 Jackson Street, St. Paul, MN 55101-3885 USA.

All photographs by Norvia Behling except for pages 13, 22, 49, 68-69, and 82, which are by Shirley Fernandez; pages 27, 29, 46-47, 86-87, and 94-95 which are by Daniel Johnson; page 32, which is by Paulette Johnson; and pages 56-57, which is by Connie Summers.

ISBN-13: 978-0-7603-2304-5
ISBN-10: 0-7603-2304-6

Editor: Amy Glaser
Designer: Mandy Iverson

Printed in China

Dogs are **miracles** with paws.

—✦—

Susan Ariel Rainbow Kennedy

A dog wags its tail

with its heart.

Martin Buxbaum

With dogs, you don't need gurus.

Dogs are forever in the moment.

They are always a tidal wave of feelings,

and *every feeling is some variant of love.*

―✢―

Cynthia Heimel

He is your *friend*,
your *partner*,
your *defender*,
your dog.
You are his *life*,
his *love*,
his *leader*.
He will be yours,
faithful and true,
to the last beat of his heart.
You owe it to him
to be worthy of such **devotion**.

—⊹—

Anonymous

The dog was created

specially for children.

He is the **god of frolic.**

Henry Ward Beecher

I can't think of anything that brings me closer to tears

than when my old dog—

completely exhausted after a hard day in the field—

limps away from her nice spot in front of the fire

and comes over to where I'm sitting

and puts her head in my lap, a paw over my knee,

and closes her eyes and goes back to sleep.

I don't know what I've done to deserve that kind of friend.

Gene Hill

I've seen a look in dogs' eyes,

a quickly vanishing *look of amazed contempt,*

and I am convinced that

basically *dogs think humans are nuts.*

John Steinbeck

Dogs have given us their absolute all. *We are the center of their universe.* We are the focus of their love and faith and trust. They serve us in return for scraps. It is without a doubt the best deal man has ever made.

Roger Caras

Scratch a dog and you'll find a *permanent job*.

※

Franklin P. Jones

If you get to thinkin' you're a *person of some influence,* try orderin' **somebody else's** dog around.

—|—

Anonymous

A really **companionable** and **indispensable** dog

is an *accident of nature*

You can't get it by breeding for it,

and you can't buy it with money.

It just happens along.

⁌

E. B. White

Blessed is the person who has **earned** the *love of an old dog.*

Sydney Jeanne Seward

Happiness is a warm puppy.

Charles M. Schulz

Dogs are not our whole life,

but *they make our lives whole.*

⁌⁍

Roger Caras

A door is what a dog is

perpetually on the *wrong side of.*

—Ogden Nash

Children and *dogs* are as **necessary** to the *welfare of the country* as *Wall Street* and the *railroads.*

—✣—

Harry S. Truman

A house *is not a* home *without a dog.*

— Anonymous

A **watchdog** is a dog kept to guard your home, usually by sleeping where a burglar **would awaken** the household by falling over him.

Anonymous

A dog is like an *eternal Peter Pan,* a *child* who never grows old and who therefore is always available to **love** and **be loved.**

Aaron Katcher

Every dog *must* have his day.

Jonathan Swift

I have found that when you are *deeply troubled* there are things you get from the *silent devoted companionship* of a dog that you can get from *no other source.*

Doris Day

What counts is not necessarily

the **size of the dog** *in the fight;*

it's the **size of the fight** *in the dog.*

⁃⊹⁃

Dwight D. Eisenhower

To *err* is *human*, to *forgive*, *canine*.

※

Anonymous

The reason dogs have so many *friends*

is because they *wag their* tails

instead of their tongues.

—✦—

Anonymous

They *never* talk about themselves,

but listen to you while you talk about yourself,

and keep up an appearance of *being interested*

in the conversation.

—✢—

Jerome R. Jerome

No matter

how little *money*

and how *few possessions*

you own,

having a **dog**

makes you **rich**.

Louis Sabin

When you feel **dog tired** at night,

it may be because you **growled** all day long.

Anonymous

I think *dogs* are the most amazing creatures; they give **unconditional love**. For me they are the role model for being alive.

Gilda Radner

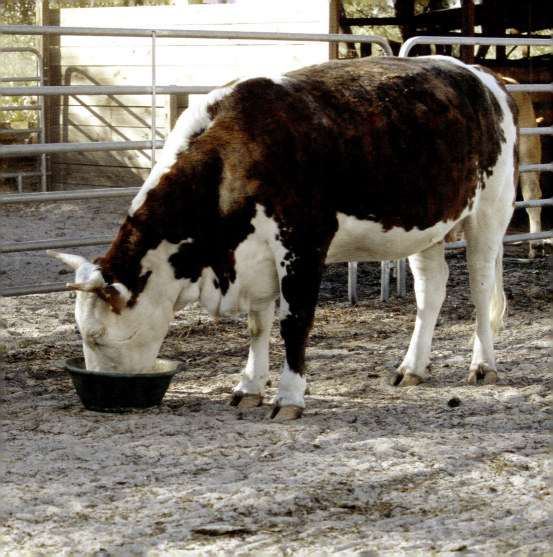

Dogs are our link to paradise.

They don't know evil or jealousy or discontent.

To sit with a dog on a hillside on a glorious afternoon

is to be back in Eden,

where doing nothing was not boring—it was **peace**.

Milan Kundera

Dogs are wise.

They crawl away into a quiet corner

and lick their wounds

and do not rejoin the world

until they are whole once more.

—✝—

Agatha Christie

Anybody who *doesn't* know

what **soap** tastes like

never **washed a dog.**

Franklin P. Jones

All knowledge,

the **totality** of all questions

and **all** answers

is *contained in the dog.*

—

Franz Kafka

When a dog **wags her tail** and **barks** at the same time,

how do you know which end to believe?

—✢—

Anonymous

They are better than

human beings

because they know

but do not tell.

Emily Dickinson

Dogs feel very strongly

that they should *always*

go with you in the car,

in case the need should arise

for them to **bark violently**

at nothing right in your ear.

―‡―

Dave Barry

There's just something about **dogs** that *makes you feel good.* You come home, they're thrilled to see you. *They're good for the ego.*

Janet Schnellman

The more people I meet, the more **I like my dog.**

—✝—

Anonymous

The fidelity of a dog is a *precious gift* demanding no less binding moral responsibilities than the friendship of a human being. *The bond with a dog is as lasting* as the ties of this earth can ever be.

— Konrad Lorenz

Money will buy you a pretty good dog, but it won't buy *the wag of his tail*.

Henry Wheeler Shaw

A barking dog is often *more useful* than **a sleeping lion.**

—I—

Washington Irving

Old dogs, like old shoes,

are comfortable.

They may be a bit out of shape

and a little worn

around the edges,

but **they fit well.**

Bonnie Wilcox

One reason *a dog* can be such a comfort

when you're *feeling blue*

is that he doesn't try to find out why.

※

Anonymous

A good dog never dies.

He always stays,

he walks beside you

on crisp autumn days

when frost is on the fields

and winter's drawing near,

his head is within our hand

in his old way.

⁌

Mary Carolyn Davies

No man can be condemned for owning a dog.

As long as he has a dog, he has a friend;

and the poorer he gets, the **better** friend he has.

Will Rogers

The average dog

is a **nicer** person

than the **average** person.

—⊹—

Andrew A. Rooney

ABOUT THE PHOTOGRAPHERS

Norvia Behling's photographs have appeared thousands of times in books, magazines, and calendars. She has been capturing the unique qualities of her subjects for 25 years. She divides her time between her farm in Wisconsin in the summers and her home in Florida in the winters. Norvia is married with one daughter.

Paulette Johnson lives with her husband and their five children on a farm in northern Wisconsin where they raise Welsh Ponies. Paulette works closely with her sister Norvia Behling in their photography pursuits. Paulette enjoys photographing farm life and horses.

Dan Johnson is able to capture on film the warmth and beauty of domestic animals of all kinds, with a special affection for horses. A horse trainer himself, Dan is able to use his understanding of these great animals to better capture their unique personalities in his beautiful portraits. Dan resides on a farm in northern Wisconsin.

Connie Summers' love of animals and passion for photography has led to her career in photography. For over 20 years Connie has photographed animals for clients worldwide. She resides in Sarasota, Florida with her husband, their two boys, two Labradors, and a Labradoodle.

Shirley Fernandez has been handling animals and fluffing fur for 15 years. She has been grooming, cleaning, and holding the animals for photographer Norvia Behling who encouraged Shirley to try her hand behind the camera. Shirley lives in Sarasota, Florida with her husband, 2 horses, 2 dogs, 10 cats, 7 chickens and many other assorted critters, and still manages to drive a school bus and meet once a week with the 4-H dog club.